LET'S BEGIN

ON THE PATH TO SCHOOL READINESS

LET'S BEGIN

ON THE PATH TO SCHOOL READINESS

Rose Marie Sicoli-Ostler

Let's Begin
San Francisco, California

Copyright © 1995

By Rose Marie Sicoli-Ostler

All rights reserved. No part of this book may be reproduced or transmitted in any form or by any means, electronic or mechanical, which includes photocopying, recording or by any information storage and retrieval system without written permission from the author, except for the inclusion of brief quotations in a review.

Let's Begin
P.O. Box 77768
San Francisco, Ca. 94107

ISBN 0-9654489-6-7

Dedicated to
my husband, Micky,
who for years encouraged me
to write this book.

Drawings: Joseph Sicoli

Cover illustration: Laura Wrede

Special thanks to
my family and many friends
who read, corrected, suggested
and encouraged.

Spend quality time with your child

CONTENTS

PAGE

Introduction	9
Talk	11
Read	15
Play	19
Development Categories	23
Cautions	25
Auditory Perception & Memory	29
Body Awareness	33
Gross Motor Skills	39
Fine Motor Skills	43
Visual Motor/Perception/Memory	45
Colors, Shapes, Sizes	49
Language & Vocabulary	53
Reading Readiness	59
Math Readiness	63
Self Awareness	69
Passage of Time	73
Structure	77
Chores & Responsibility	79
Television Time	81
Socialization	85
Nutrition	89
Sleep	91
School Attendance	93
Readiness Survey	95
Home Supplies	99
Additional Ideas	101

Children are precious and should be valued

PREPARING YOUR CHILD FROM BIRTH TO KINDERGARTEN FOR A SUCCESSFUL SCHOOL EXPERIENCE

Parents are not only their children's first teacher they can also be their best. Almost every living creature must be nurtured and educated by one or both parents. Observing most animals, you will notice they teach by showing. You, too, can teach by example. How fortunate we are to be able to use language also.

After a few years of teaching Kindergarten, it was very easy during the first few weeks of school to know which children had been introduced to their surroundings, which had been encouraged to learn and which had been stimulated from birth to five years old. The children who came from homes where the environment was challenging and nurturing were not only eager to start school but were very ready to learn.

Unfortunately, it was also very clear which children had been given little or no attention during the first five years of their lives. Those who had not heard much conversation, spent too many hours in front of a television set, who had not been introduced to books and reading, who had limited life experiences and were denied general good care began Kindergarten with many strikes against them. At five years old they were already lagging behind and I knew they would have a rough road ahead of them.

DON'T LET THIS HAPPEN TO YOUR CHILD!

As a parent, there is much that you can do to ensure that your child will be ready to begin school and that it will be a wonderful experience for you both. Believe it or not, it is quite easy and fun to do. Best of all it requires no special talent, no special tools and no expensive materials. All it takes is a little time each day along with love, care and attention. Even if you are a working parent, you can make a difference in your child's readiness for school.

> **MAKE YOUR CHILD A PRIORITY IN YOUR LIFE.**

Everything you do with your youngster will affect his or her success in school. The greater the experience, the easier the learning. The more you help your youngster to participate in the activities described on the following pages, the easier school will be.

The benefits will be better if you start at birth; but remember it is never too late.

You can assure that your child gets on the proper path to school readiness.
So.......

TALK– TALK–TALK

From <u>birth</u> on, talk, talk, talk. Talk to your child every chance you get.

Talk to your infant while you are

- Changing diapers
- Dressing
- Feeding

Tell your baby

- What you are doing
- What is happening
- About your plans for the day

Tell your son or daughter about

- The weather
- The color & designs on clothes
- The food you are cooking

Tell your child

- About the groceries you are buying
- About the train trip you will take
- About your garden

Talk to your baby just as you would an adult. Use the same expressions when speaking to your baby that you would when speaking with a friend.

Talk, Talk, Talk...

- In a soothing tone
- In an exciting tone
- In a fun tone
- In a friendly tone

Speak to your child the moment he or she is born. You will marvel at the attention given you. Soon your baby will be communicating back to you with cooing, movement and facial expressions.

You will also want to provide as much visual and sensory stimulation for your baby as possible. Colors, shapes and pictures around the crib, play area and infant seat will also aid in the learning process. Safe mobiles are wonderful for hanging over the crib. They provide colors, movement, shapes and sometimes music.

Please remember to use safe objects.

We all know a child learns to talk by hearing others speak. When speaking to your son or daughter, use complete sentences. Use expressive, descriptive words. When your child talks to you, asks you questions or speaks with you, respond in complete sentences; don't answer yes or no or with one word. Do not be afraid to use big words as you can explain their meaning. The more words you use, the better developed your child's vocabulary will be.

Talking builds vocabulary which, in turn, builds an understanding of words. Words have one basic purpose: communication. If your child has good communication skills, all other phases of learning will be much easier.

Verbalizing about every part of your life, home, family, community and the world will start your child on an exciting journey of learning and success.

Talking costs nothing. It is one of the best tools you can give your child. Start now.

TALKING TO YOUR CHILD FROM BIRTH WILL BE THE FIRST STEP YOU TAKE AS YOUR CHILD'S BEST TEACHER.

When you introduce your child to books you introduce the world

READ–READ–READ

As soon as your infant is <u>six months old</u> begin to read, read, read.

Reading to your child, as well as talking, will be the most important activity you do to prepare your youngster for school. At least once a day, read a good book to your son or daughter. Use books with lots of colorful pictures. As you are reading, point out and talk about the pictures, drawings or photographs. There are terrific books available for ages as young as six months.

The library is a wonderful source for children's books. When your baby is <u>six months old</u> begin making regular visits to your local library and ask the librarian to show you the location of books appropriate for your child's age. Some libraries have special programs for children in all age groups. When visiting my neighborhood library, I have seen mothers with babies on their laps sitting in the children's section listening to the librarian reading a story. Active babies do not seem to be a distraction. If you have one, talk to your librarian.

As your youngster gets older, encourage him to choose the books which you take home from the library. Teach proper care for the borrowed books. Taking your youngster to the library at an early age enhances preparation for school learning and serves as an introduction to what can become a lifelong, rewarding experience.

The world can be at your child's fingertips through the use of books.

Reading to your child provides a perfect opportunity for closeness and cuddling. Find a quiet, comfortable spot, put your baby or toddler on your lap and spend a few valuable moments together. It is time you will cherish and remember fondly for years.

Once upon a time................

As you are reading, occasionally run your hand over the words going from left to right. This will help your child begin to understand the process we use to read.

When your child is old enough, about <u>a year and one half</u>, ask him to point to specific objects. For example, ask your toddler to point to something in the picture such as the dog, the sun or the grass. If your child does not know what it is you are asking, point it out and say: "This is the grass." Take this opportunity to talk about the color of grass, where we find grass and what grass feels like.

When your child begins to speak, you can ask questions about the picture such as:

- What is the little girl playing with?
- What is the daddy doing?
- Where are the ducks going?

Children take great delight in having a book read over and over. While it requires a great deal of patience on your part, the results are invaluable. Repetition is an important key to learning. Because you have done this, your son or daughter will have the story memorized. He or she may want to pretend to read the book to you. Encourage this activity. As your child gets older, <u>four years</u> on, have her tell you the story in her own words. She can do this while looking at the pictures and turning the pages.

Reading to your youngster will also begin the listening process. When you ask questions while you read, your child will begin to understand that listening is important. You can even help this process by telling your son or daughter to let you know when they hear a specific word or when something happens. Such as, "Tell me when you hear me read about the girl's grandmother."

As your child gets older and expresses an interest in a particular subject, suggest that you both learn more about it by finding a book in the library. This will help your child develop the understanding that books are a place where information can be found.

If you do nothing else with your child, find a few moments to read together. Your youngster will be much more successful in school when you do this simple task.

Besides it's fun, simple and free.

> READING TO YOUR CHILDREN FROM SIX MONTHS ON WILL GIVE THEM A HEAD START ON LEARNING HOW TO READ AND WRITE.

PLAY- PLAY- PLAY

From <u>birth</u> on, play, play, play. Play is an important factor in your child's development. Through play your child will develop small and large muscles, hand-eye coordination, problem solving, social skills, an awareness of his surroundings and much, much more.

As was suggested in the section on talking, begin playing with your infant at <u>birth</u>. Play with your infant while

- changing a diaper
- bathing
- sitting
- whenever possible.

Usually, babies are cheerful and happy when they awake from a nap. What a special time to take a moment and play with your infant. It is a perfect time for bonding and enjoying your little one.

Crawling is a very important phase of development. Do not discourage your baby from crawling. Give her ample room to crawl, explore, touch and reach out for toys. Do not always make it easy and hand it over. This is also part of learning.

When your baby is crawling, get down on the floor and play with your little one. Encourage her to crawl to you. Hold out a favorite toy, shake a rattle, roll a ball. Get down on your stomach and get eye to eye with your son or daughter. Watch with delight as he or she responds to you.

When your toddler plays with toys, you play too. Get involved in her play. What a great time to do a lot of talking too.

Keep in mind it is not necessary to have expensive toys. Children love cardboard boxes and household items such as pots and pans.

As the child gets older, color and do puzzles together. Get in the pretend mode.

This is not to say that you should be with your youngster every minute. A child must learn to play alone and with other children; but it is important that parents spend time in play with their children.

As soon as your child is old enough, visit the park and encourage use of the playground equipment. Be sure that your youngster plays on the equipment appropriate for his age group. All the climbing opportunities encountered on the playground will assist in the development of your son or daughter.

Play ball with your child. Roll it, kick it, catch it, throw it. Your toddler will take great delight in chasing after the ball.

If you can make them available, encourage tricycle/bicycle riding and skating which aid in the development of coordination.

More ideas and information will follow on ways to help in the development and formation of large and fine muscles, hand-eye coordination and coordination in general.

It is important to keep in mind that play is very important in a child's development and readiness for school. A qualified kindergarten teacher can easily identify those children who have, in the first five years of their lives, spent time in play. It is obvious which children have played with adults, other children and who have learned to play well alone.

GIVE YOUR CHILD MANY OPPORTUNITIES TO PLAY WITH YOU, OTHER CHILDREN AND ALONE.

Children are very observant
Encourage their curiosity

CATEGORIES

There are many activities to which your child must be exposed in order to be ready for school and learning. Some categories and a short description are listed below. Details on ways to work with your child in each area are described more fully on the following pages.

<u>AUDITORY PERCEPTION & MEMORY:</u> Ability to hear and identify sounds, differences between words, rhyming words, etc. Also hear, recall and respond to a command.

<u>BODY AWARENESS:</u> Ability to name & know parts of the body. Know and feel the relation of the body to the space around.

<u>COLORS:</u> Knows the names of and recognizes basic colors.

<u>FINE MOTOR:</u> Development of small muscles.

<u>GROSS MOTOR:</u> Development of large muscles and coordination.

<u>LANGUAGE DEVELOPMENT:</u> Being able to express self appropriately, speak clearly and have good vocabulary skills.

LOCATION & DIRECTION: Understanding positions such as: on, outside, above, on the top, on the bottom, middle, right, etc.

MATH READINESS: Knows the names of and recognizes some numbers from 1-10. Able to count to at least 5 or 10. (Also see the categories of shapes & sizes, and location & direction).

PASSAGE OF TIME: Understanding days, weeks, years, morning, evening, hours in the day and seasons.

READING READINESS: Knows the names of and recognizes some letters of the alphabet. Understands the value of reading and books. (Also see the categories of auditory perception & memory, visual motor, visual perception & memory).

SELF AWARENESS: A sense of self, self-confidence, self-esteem and one's place in the world.

SHAPES: Knows the names of and recognizes shapes such as circle, square, rectangle, and triangle.

SIZES: Knows concepts such as largest, smallest, tall, short, etc.

VISUAL MOTOR: Ability to copy letters or designs, cut or follow a line, hold a pencil or crayon properly.

VISUAL PERCEPTION & MEMORY: Ability to see things as they are and find similar or different objects. Also recall or reproduce from memory.

IMPORTANT

DO THE ACTIVITIES SUGGESTED ON THE FOLLOWING PAGES

IN A FUN, RELAXED WAY

WHICH WAY SHOULD IT BE?

 THE FOLLOWING PAGES SET DOWN SOME OF THE WAYS IN WHICH YOU CAN HELP YOUR CHILD DEVELOP AND BE READY FOR A SUCCESSFUL SCHOOL EXPERIENCE. AS MENTIONED ON THE PREVIOUS PAGE, DO THE ACTIVITIES IN A FUN AND RELAXED MANNER. DO NOT MAKE IT A "CHORE" OR A "HAVE TO" ACTIVITY. KEEP THE TIME SHORT.

REMEMBER: A CHILD'S ATTENTION SPAN IS LIMITED.

PLEASE TAKE SPECIAL NOTE OF THE APPROPRIATE AGE GROUPS FOR EACH ACTIVITY.

DO NOT PUSH YOUR CHILD TO LEARN SUBJECTS THAT ARE TOO ADVANCED FOR HIS OR HER AGE.

IF YOU SPEND AT LEAST 20 OR 30 MINUTES EVERY DAY WITH YOUR YOUNGSTER, EITHER WORKING ON THE ACTIVITIES SUGGESTED, OR JUST ENJOYING YOUR CHILD, THE BENEFITS WILL BE UNLIMITED (BOTH TO YOU AND YOUR CHILD). GIVE YOUR BOY OR GIRL THE OPPORTUNITY TO SUCCEED. CHILDREN ARE EAGER TO LEARN AND ARE VERY, VERY CAPABLE.

LEARNING SHOULD BE FUN!

ACTIVITIES & IDEAS

The following pages contain activities for each of the categories listed on the previous pages. Hopefully, the ideas suggested will be just a start. Once you understand the appropriate activities for each area, you will be creative and develop many of your own.

Do not do any of the activities over and over for long periods of time. Try to do a little each day and, of course, only the activities which are suitable for your child's age.

The more you do as part of everyday life, the better it will be. Leave "formal lessons" for the teachers and school.

HAVE FUN.

Children are like little sponges
They soak up all the information
you can give

AUDITORY PERCEPTION & MEMORY

From <u>birth</u> talk, talk, talk and read, read, read to your child. Just hearing words and sounds begins the auditory perception and memory process. When your child starts school, this skill will be important for phonics, reading and all other subject matter. The more you read and talk to your baby, toddler and child, the easier it will be for him to learn to talk and, of course, read and learn.

As your toddler begins to talk, he will automatically try to repeat what you say. You can encourage speaking by saying a word such as "dog" and talking about a dog. Your youngster will probably make an attempt to say dog. <u>Whatever response is given should be praised</u>. Repeat this process during the day whenever it is appropriate and there is time. It should not be a lesson; it should be just part of your normal day.

As you go through the day with your son or daughter, listen for sounds and call them to his or her attention; such as, hearing a train whistle, a car horn, a bird chirp. Say to your baby: Do you hear the:

- train whistle
- car horn
- bird chirp
- dog barking
- wind whistling through the trees

You can even mimic the sound so that your baby or toddler knows what you are hearing. Help your child become aware of all the sounds that surround us.

There are many sounds in your home such as the

- clock ticking (they can't all be digital)
- refrigerator motor
- washing machine
- water running
- and many more

Talk about the sounds you hear, what the object is doing and what purpose it has. For example, "Do you hear the refrigerator motor?" "It is working to keep the food cold so it does not spoil." In this way your child has been exposed to sound, science, engineering and vocabulary. All this learning will take place with just a few moments of conversation.

After you have read a story, encourage your son or daughter to tell you the story in his or her own words. Age <u>three</u> and on is appropriate for this activity.

A fun game you can do is say a series of words or numbers and have your child repeat them. Start with two words or two numbers and work your way up. This encourages listening.

From <u>four to six years</u>, continue the activities previously mentioned and add the following:

- Rhythmic clapping is a good exercise. You clap out a rhythm and see if your child can repeat it. Make sure you do very simple ones until your youngster understands the process. This can be fun if you are creative and allow your child to be successful.

- You can create any type of sound with any object; doing it in such a way that your child can copy. At first, do everything in a simple manner so that your youngster will be successful and more inclined to want to continue.

- Give your child a simple direction such as "Please shut the door and come here." Increase the complexity of directions to include 2 or 3 things, such as "Get the banana, please. Give it to me and watch me peel it." Listening and memory are necessary for this activity.

Be sure not to show disappointment or frustration if your child is not able to do things perfectly. Encourage and praise are always important.

- Teach your child rhymes and stories which he or she can repeat.

- Tell your child a story and have him repeat it.

- Teach your youngster her address and telephone number.

- Listening is part of everyday life and very important for school readiness.

TEACH YOUR CHILD TO LISTEN TO THE WONDERFUL SOUNDS WHICH SURROUND US ALL. A CHILD WHO LEARNS TO LISTEN AND HEAR WILL BE BETTER PREPARED FOR SCHOOL.

BODY AWARENESS

It is important that your child be able to identify the parts of the body and know the proper name for each. This will provide a very good foundation for the development of self and who and where he is in relation to the world.

You can begin this when your child is just a <u>few months old</u>. While you are holding, cuddling, dressing, or changing a diaper, gently touch your child's nose and say, "This is your nose." Hold her two hands, clap them together and say "These are your hands." Each day mention a different body part.

When the child is older and begins to take verbal direction, make a game out of asking "Where is your nose?" "Show me your feet." "Touch your elbows." If your child does not know or is confused, be sure to show her by example. Touch your elbows and say "These are my elbows, where are yours?" Whenever you do something like this it should be fun and last only for a few minutes. Do not make this a lesson.

At age <u>three</u>, you can ask your child to name the parts of the body. Touch her nose and say "What is this?" Again, if your child does not know the name, you name it and have your youngster repeat it. An ideal time to do this is while you are dressing your youngster or while your child sits on your lap and cuddles.

At least once a week when I taught Kindergarten, I would do the following activity:

I would ask the children to:

- Stand and put both hands on the top of your head.

- Now run them down over your ears and place them on the side of your neck.

- Go out to your shoulders, down under your arm and down your torso to your waist.

- Squeeze your waist and then run your hands down over your hips and down the thighs.

- Place your hands on your knees, down your leg to your ankles.

- Now run your hands over your feet and touch your toes.

Another day we would play the "Simon Says" game saying: "Simon Says" touch your nose. "Simon Says" touch your knees. I would continue the game until all parts of the body had been mentioned. The children who did not know the correct part of the body would learn by watching others. You can assist your child's learning by placing your hands on the specific parts of your body as you call out their names.

You can create games of your own and your child will love them. As your child becomes more skilled, have her close her eyes and do it. This will help her become aware of her body in space and the body parts in relationship with one another.

Fingerplays are a wonderful way to help your youngster become aware of his or her body. Here are just a few that I used while teaching. The movements for each are obvious:

I am a rubber person.
I stretch and stretch as far as I can.
I stretch my neck, I stretch my hands,
I stretch my legs like rubber-bands.
And then the stretch goes out of me,
And I'm as limp as I can be.

****

This is my right hand.
This is my left hand.
Together they come and clap, clap, clap.

This is my right hand.
This is my left hand.
Together they come and sit on my lap.

****

I'll touch my hair, my lips, my eyes.
I'll sit up straight, then I'll rise.
I'll touch my ears, my nose, my chin,
Then quietly sit down again.

* * * * * * *

My hands upon my hips I place
On my shoulders, on my face,
On my knees and at my side,
Then behind me they would hide.
Then I raise them up so high,
Swiftly let my fingers fly.
Quickly count one, two, three
And see how quiet they can be.
(bring hands down to lap)

Parts of the body your child should know are:

HEAD
    EYES
        EARS
            NOSE
                MOUTH
                    NECK
SHOULDERS
        ARMS
            ELBOWS
                WRISTS
                    HANDS
                        FINGERS
CHEST
    BACK
        WAIST
            HIPS
                THIGHS
                    KNEES

ANKLES
    FEET
        TOES

AN AWARENESS OF BODY HELPS YOUR CHILD IN ALL OTHER ASPECTS OF LEARNING AND SCHOOL READINESS.

GROSS MOTOR SKILLS (LARGE MUSCLES)

You can assist in the development of your child's gross motor skills (large muscles) by encouraging play as much as possible. Good coordination enhances learning, reading and writing skills.

Give your <u>baby</u> the freedom to move. You can gently move her arms and legs when dressing and changing her diapers. As she begins to crawl, allow her the space to do so. Have safe toys which she can reach for, grasp and hold. The toys should be small enough to hold, but not small enough to swallow.

At about <u>a year and one half or two</u>, begin to roll a large rubber ball to your child. She can easily learn to pick it up and roll it back to you. As she gets older, throw the ball, bounce the ball and play catch.

Playing ball also helps your youngster develop hand-eye coordination.

Give your baby and toddler every opportunity to move and explore. While you must be sensible and careful, don't discourage a baby from crawling up and down stairs. They are developing their muscles and understanding spatial relationship.

Large blocks are great objects for large muscle development. Naturally, small blocks will help develop small muscles also.

You can make your own by collecting pieces of wood of different sizes and shapes at your local carpentry shop or lumber mill. You might have to sand them to make them smooth. Garage sales and second-hand stores are a great source for children's equipment.

Take your children to a safe, well equipped park and allow them to crawl around on the equipment. Make sure you watch that they use apparatus which is age appropriate.

At <u>24 to 30 months</u>, show your tot how to jump, hop on one foot, and skip. Running usually comes naturally.

Old automobile tires are great for crawling over and into. Jumping in and out of a tire is a terrific activity for developing muscles and coordination.

Make music available in your home.

March and dance around the room with your child. While there is an ample supply of children's tapes available for marching, exercise and dancing, it is not necessary to get the "best that money can buy." Just turn on your radio or, better yet, be creative and let your child be creative.

Household items make wonderful instruments. Using common, everyday products will also help your child develop imagination. Oatmeal boxes make wonderful drums. Paper towel tubes can become horns. Pot lids can be cymbals. A little noise can be tolerated when you realize you are encouraging creativity.

Another super activity is jumping rope; however, it is a little more difficult. <u>Five years old</u> is probably the proper age to introduce a jump rope.

Helping with chores around the house will also build strong muscles. Let your child help you with:

- gardening
- cleaning the house
- doing dishes
- carrying groceries
- sweeping
- folding towels
- washing the car
- putting away toys
- dusting

You will not only be providing a means for your child to develop gross motor skills and hand-eye coordination, but you will be teaching good life skills.

Remember each child develops at a different pace.

Do not push a child who is not ready for a particular activity.

BLOCKS, BALLS, PLAYGROUNDS, MUSIC AND HOUSEHOLD CHORES BUILD MUSCLES AND DEVELOP COORDINATION.

FINE MOTOR SKILLS (SMALL MUSCLES)

Obviously, developing a child's small muscles will be important for writing skills. As with large muscle development, <u>infants</u> should have toys or objects available that they can grab and hold with their tiny hands.

REMEMBER, NOT SO TINY THAT THEY MIGHT SWALLOW

Let your toddler color and scribble. Provide safe pencils, crayons and paper. You can use coloring books but do not obsess about staying in the lines. This will come naturally as your child gets older— about <u>four or five</u>. As her small muscles and hand-eye coordination develop she will be able to do it.

Play dough or child's clay (non-toxic) is a marvelous product for strengthening hand muscles. Allow your child to play and create... her little fingers will develop and grow strong. This activity is appropriate for children <u>three years</u> and older.

Tracing and connecting dots can be fun for <u>four and five year olds</u>. There are wonderful workbooks available for these activities; however, you can make worksheets yourself. For instance, place a series of dots on a page and show your youngster how to connect them. Use your imagination and create a picture.

When I mention using workbooks or worksheets, it is meant as a suggestion for materials. They should not be used as <u>WORK</u> BOOKS. If you use them, let your child explore and have fun. You can show your youngster what to do on each page, but do not turn it into a lesson and have your child feel bad because she MADE A MISTAKE.

The next section contains activities which will also develop fine motor skills.

YOUR CHILD WILL BE PREPARED TO HOLD A PENCIL IF YOU GIVE MANY OPPORTUNITIES TO DEVELOP SMALL MUSCLES.

VISUAL MOTOR
VISUAL PERCEPTION
VISUAL MEMORY

The gross and fine motor skills described on the previous pages will also play a part in the development of a child's visual motor, perception and memory skills.

When your son or daughter is pre-kindergarten, <u>four and one-half to five years</u>, you can introduce additional activities such as: cutting pictures out of magazines and pasting them on a piece of paper.

<u>USE CHILDREN'S SAFETY SCISSORS</u>

<u>NO SHARP, POINTED, ADULT SCISSORS</u>.

Stringing beads or uncooked salad macaroni is a great activity.

You can begin to teach your child to tie shoelaces at this age.....

<u>you will need</u>

<u>PATIENCE, PATIENCE, PATIENCE!</u>

Always praise the effort. Never scold a child who is trying.

At age four and one-half to five, you can add the following type of activities:

Collect various objects such as

- cotton
- sandpaper
- dirt
- paper
- different types of material such as velvet, corduroy, flannel.

Have your youngster feel the items and describe how they feel. Use terms such as soft, rough, smooth.

After you have done this several times, you can have her close her eyes, feel the object and tell you what she thinks it is.

Collect objects from around the house:

- pencils
- pens
- fruit
- vegetables
- spoons
- forks
- and more

Ask your son or daughter what objects go together. Example: pens and pencils and paper belong together because you can write or draw with them. Bananas, apples and oranges match because they are all fruit.

It's important that you respect your child's answer..even if it is not what you expect. If the youngster puts a piece of paper with the banana and apple, do not say "you are wrong." Ask your child to explain why he or she put the paper with the fruit. You might be surprised at how logical the answer will be. You might say, "That is a very good reason, but the paper should go with the pen and pencil because they are all objects which we use to write or draw." "The banana, apple and orange are all fruit which we can eat."

Use this process with all activities. You want to help your youngster to learn how to do things properly; but you don't want to intimidate or discourage him or her from trying.

Children can cut pictures out of magazines and classify them such as people, houses, cars, furniture. You can make a design with blocks or peg boards and ask your child to copy it. As a child understands the concept and becomes skillful, you can make the design, let her look at it, hide it and have her try to duplicate it.

Puzzles are also excellent for the development of visual perception. Start with puzzles which have just a few large pieces. Those with smaller and more pieces can be used as your child gets older and progresses.

> **VISUAL PERCEPTION ACTIVITIES WILL GIVE YOUR CHILD A HEAD START ON LEARNING TO DECIPHER LETTERS AND WORDS.**

Be there for your child

COLORS, SHAPES, SIZES

Knowing colors, shapes and sizes is important for school readiness.

It's so simple to teach these concepts....just talk about them from <u>birth to five years old.</u>

- When dressing your baby, toddler or youngster, talk about the color of his clothes.

- Whenever you are playing with your youngster, mention the color of the toy.

- If you are outside taking a walk, talk about the colors in nature: beautiful blue sky, soft green grass, wonderful yellow flowers, happy brown birds, fluffy white clouds, etc.

Notice the use of the adjectives to describe the object...<u>beautiful</u> blue sky. You will be accomplishing two objectives here. You will be teaching color as well as expressive language.

You can do the same thing for sizes.

Say:

- "Look at the <u>LITTLE</u> flower."

- "Do you see the <u>TALL</u> buildings?"

- "One rabbit is <u>LARGE</u> and the other rabbit is <u>SMALL</u>."

You can make your child aware of shapes in the same manner as you do colors and sizes. Shapes are all around us. If you are aware, your child will be too.

- "Do you see the round sign?"

- "Look at the moon. It is a circle."

- "The box you are playing with is a square."

- "The cracker you are eating is a rectangle."

- "Do you see the sign in the shape of a triangle?"

(Sizes and shapes will be discussed again in the math readiness section.)

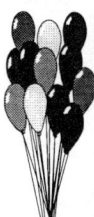

YOUR CHILD'S WORLD IS FULL OF BEAUTIFUL COLORS, WONDERFUL OBJECTS IN ALL SHAPES AND SIZES. GIVE THIS TREMENDOUS GIFT TO YOUR YOUNGSTER.

*Children have much to say
Include them in conversation*

LANGUAGE AND VOCABULARY DEVELOPMENT

The more your son or daughter hears words, the greater will be language development and vocabulary.

The greater a child's language development and the larger a child's vocabulary, the better prepared the girl or boy will be for school. As was mentioned at the beginning of this book,

READ—READ—READ

TALK—TALK—TALK

When reading to your child, talk about words. Discuss their sounds and meanings. If you come upon a word that your youngster may not understand, ask if she knows the meaning. You might be surprised and will probably have fun with her explanation. If she does not understand, provide the meaning.

Be careful in your reaction if you are given the wrong meaning.

<u>Do not make your child feel she is wrong or has made a mistake.</u>

You want to avoid discouraging her for the next time.

Talk to your youngster in complete sentences and encourage her to answer completely. If your daughter has been visiting a friend and you ask, "Did you have fun?" and she answers, "Yes," try to continue the conversation. Ask your child "What did you do?" Ask questions that will require full answers.

There are many activities which cost very little, if anything at all, and will develop your child's language and vocabulary.

Don't wait for a time when you have to travel...take your child to the

- park
- bus station
- train depot
- subway
- zoo
- aquarium
- museum
- art gallery
- beach
- tourist spots
- college science centers
- nature centers
- historical sites

Show your youngster all the activities at each location. Use the proper words when discussing the employees and activities. For instance, the airport provides a wealth of vocabulary opportunities:

- reservation clerk
- baggage handlers
- mechanics
- tourists
- jet engine
- flaps, wings
- baggage carousel
- automobile rentals
- vendors
- restaurants
- shuttle buses
- vacations
- and many, many more words

Imagine how much your children will learn about animals if you take them to the zoo. If they were to just look at the animals, with absolutely no conversation, some learning would take place.

Consider how much greater the learning is when the animals, their food, their habitat, their sounds and unique activities which you both observe are discussed.

Your children will learn many new words and many new facts.

GIRAFFE

HIBERNATE

GROWL

Introduce your child to

ART MUSIC SCIENCE

There are many facilities and activities available to children that cost little or nothing. A few examples are: museums, art galleries, city or town musical events, observatories, and planetariums.

Check the front of the yellow pages of your telephone book. Some list the locations of these places in your city.

A visit to these exhibits and sites will not only increase your child's vocabulary, but will enrich his or her life immensely.

> A LARGE VOCABULARY AND GOOD VERBAL SKILLS WILL INCREASE YOUR CHILD'S CHANCES FOR SUCCESS IN SCHOOL.

Children are eager to learn

READING READINESS

Reading readiness begins at <u>birth</u>. When you talk to your child, you are preparing her for reading; however, the most valuable and significant activity you can do is

<u>READ to your infant, child and youngster.</u>

Reading to your child is probably the most important activity you will do to prepare your child for reading, overall learning and school.

At <u>six months</u> you should begin to read to your baby. As you hold him in your arms, take a picture book, read the story and talk about the pictures. Point to the picture of a ball and say, "See the ball; it is round, green and it bounces." Of course you will use very colorful picture books which are available for small children. Continue this as your child grows and develops...always using books appropriate for your youngster's age.

At a _year and one half_, include the process of asking your toddler to point to a specific object.

- Show me the ball.
- Show me the dog.
- Where is the boat?

If you have been reading to your child from an early age, at _three_ your child should be able to pretend to read the story to you. If it is one that is familiar, he will probably be able to tell you the story while turning the pages. If it is an unfamiliar book, one with lots of pictures, encourage him to make up the story based on the pictures.

At _three_, point out the words as you read. Show him the picture of the dog and then point to the word dog. Say:

- This is a picture of a dog.
- This is the word that says dog.

Your child will begin to understand that there is a written word for an object.

If you do nothing more than read to your child, you will do much for his reading readiness as well as general school readiness. You should continue reading to your child even after he goes to school. Children love the closeness it brings.

When the student learns to read, it is important that you sit and listen while he reads aloud. Do this every evening.

Other activities you can do include the following:

When your child reaches three and one half to four, label objects around the house such as

- chair
- table
- television
- bed
- radio
- any other item in your home

Children will learn by sight the word for the object. As you are walking or riding around town, or when visiting a store, talk about signs you see. Point out a stop sign and tell your youngster that the sign says "Stop." Guess who will soon be "reading" the sign that says "Stop?"

At this same age ask questions about a story you have read.

- What happened to the little girl when she ran in the street?
- What do you think she should have done?
- Was it a good idea to run in the street after the ball?

These activities will begin the process of reading comprehension, understanding sequence of events, and ability to predict outcome. All these processes are important for good reading skills.

<u>Three and four</u> is a good age to talk about the letters; point out the "a" and say its name. Do this with all the letters. Ask your child to show you an "a", "x", "o". Your youngster will learn the alphabet without study or structure.

At <u>four to five</u>, (or even earlier) talk about the meaning of words, the content of the story and encourage thinking, planning and predicting by asking questions such as:

- Do you have other ideas on how the boy could have fixed his bike?

- How would you solve the boy's problem?

- What would you have done?

If you wish and feel comfortable doing it, you can talk about the sounds of a letter. This is an "s" and it says "ssss". Once a child learns all the sounds of the letters, sounding out a word will be much easier. Phonics is a major factor in learning to read. If you do not really know the sounds of each vowel and consonant, it is probably best to leave this area to the teacher and school.

**IF YOU DO NOTHING ELSE
READ, READ, READ
TO YOUR CHILD.**

MATH READINESS

5　　**8**　　　$2+2=4$
　　　　3　　　　　　　1

Math readiness also begins at an <u>early age.</u> Talk about numbers just as you would letters and words. There are number books appropriate for children from <u>six months on.</u> The first page usually has a large number one and then a picture of one object. You can read this with your tot and say: "See the <u>one</u>." Point to the number and then say: "This is <u>one</u> ball." Children will grow up understanding the concept of the number <u>one</u> and the fact that it stands for <u>one</u> object.

At age <u>two,</u> ask your toddler to show you the correct number of objects for each number; such as: "Show me two spoons." Understanding this concept usually begins when you ask a two year old "How old are you?" and he or she has learned to hold up two fingers.

Try to use numbers in general conversation. You might say to your son or daughter:

- Can you get mommy her two shoes?
- Will you bring daddy his four keys on the key ring?
- Please get five forks and spoons.
- Let's get two loaves of bread.

Whenever possible, show your child the written number that corresponds to the number you are discussing.

At <u>two & one half to three,</u> if you have not already done so, point out to your youngster shapes such as circles, squares, triangles, rectangles, ovals, curves, corners. Find these shapes in the house and outdoors. Ask your child the shape of a ball. Look for things in the shape of squares and rectangles. You can use household objects such as buttons, crackers, picture frames, a sponge or napkins (fold in half for a triangle). Use your imagination.

From <u>three years on</u>, let your child help set the table. Talk about the fact that you have five members in the family and need five plates, five forks, five napkins, and five glasses.

When children understand the concept of numbers, they will have a much easier time learning and understanding that $2 + 5 = 7$.

Begin this process by making sets of objects such as a set of two pencils; a set of five pencils. Then you can show your child what happens when you put the two pencils with the five pencils. Now you have seven pencils.

When it comes time to add numbers, it will be much easier as your child will understand the concept of putting groups of objects and/or numbers together.

Dominos can be used for matching by putting the same number of dots side by side. They can also be used for counting.

Number bingo is fun. You can make bingo cards using numbers instead of letters.

Any type of matching will prepare your child for math. You can encourage your child to match items of the same

- color
- shape
- size

Fabric stores and second-hand shops sell buttons of all sizes, shapes and colors. You can buy a couple of dozen and have your child sort by color, shape and size.

THIS IS NOT A SUITABLE ACTIVITY FOR TODDLERS.

THEY MAY SWALLOW THE BUTTON.

USE THIS ACTIVITY FOR <u>FOUR</u> AND <u>FIVE</u> YEAR OLDS ONLY.

Classifying is another important skill necessary for school readiness:

Put out items such as pieces of fruit, kitchen utensils, and clothing. Have your child sort by category; that is, put all the fruit in one pile, the kitchen utensils together and all the clothing in another pile.

Understanding the order in which we do things will help with math as well as reading comprehension.

In what order do we get ready for school?

- get out of bed
- get dressed
- eat breakfast
- put on a jacket
- walk to school

Before we go to bed we:

- take a bath
- put on our pajamas
- brush our teeth
- get into bed
- go to sleep

Develop the concepts of first, middle, last. If you have three children, you can talk about who is first, who is in the middle, who was born last.

Put three objects down in a row and discuss the object that is in the middle, which one is first (going left to right) and which one is last. Put three children in a line. Have the first child raise her hand, then the middle, and the last.

If your children understand the concepts of the following terms they will be better prepared to learn math in school.

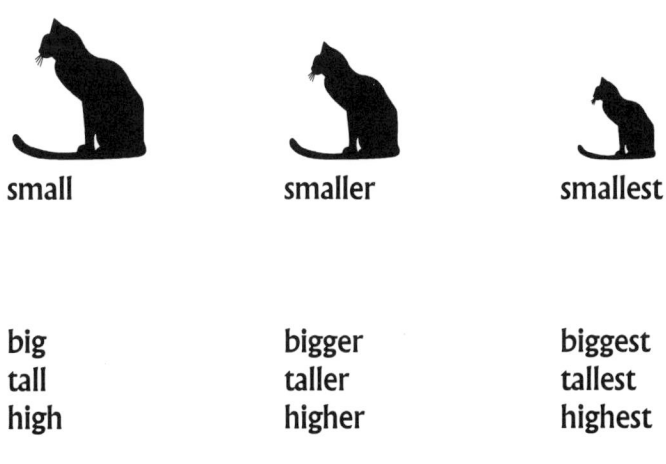

| small | smaller | smallest |

big	bigger	biggest
tall	taller	tallest
high	higher	highest

...you get the idea.

More terms are:

above	between	below
over	under	across
up	down	beneath
left	right	first
last	same	different
open	close	on
off	top	middle
bottom	inside	outside
short	long	hard
soft	heavy	light
next to	beside	in front
behind		

The list is endless. It is important that you use these words in everyday conversation as often as you can. Begin at birth.

CHILDREN CAN BE TAUGHT MATH CONCEPTS USING REGULAR DAILY ACTIVITIES. ALL IT TAKES IS A LITTLE AWARENESS AND THOUGHT ON YOUR PART.

SELF AWARENESS

One of the most important aspects of a child's learning and readiness skills is awareness of <u>SELF.</u>

WHO AM I?
WHAT DO I LOOK LIKE?
WHO ARE THE MEMBERS OF MY FAMILY?

A child's awareness of self, self-confidence, self-esteem, and sense of security begins at <u>BIRTH</u>. Love, tenderness, cuddling, talking and playing begin a baby's process of developing self-awareness and a healthy self-concept.

Treat your child with the same respect you would give another adult or friend. In order for your child to become aware of self, talk about his appearance.

- What beautiful red hair you have.
- Look at your brown eyes.
- My, how tall you are getting.

Recently, I had the opportunity to chat with a two year old girl I did not know. During our conversation I said to her "You have beautiful eyes." She responded immediately and said with great pride, "My eyes are green." Her parents know what it takes to instill self-awareness and self-esteem in a child.

As a toddler reaches <u>two</u>, talk about feelings.

- I know you are feeling angry right now.
- Oh, you seem so happy today!
- I know it's sad when daddy goes to work.

Children need to know that all the feelings we have such as: anger, sadness, happiness, fear, are normal and okay. When you talk about their feelings and teach your children how to deal with them, they will have a much healthier attitude about Self.

Talk about family. You cannot start too early.

- See what your brother is doing.
- Grandma is coming to visit tomorrow.
- Your cousin started school today.
- Uncle Jim is going on a trip.

Give your child as much opportunity as possible to spend time with the extended family. Make a family tree with pictures of grandparents, aunts, uncles, cousins. This will aid in your child's understanding of all the members of a family.

Help your child understand about his home, house or apartment. Talk about your living space. At <u>two and one-half to three</u> teach your youngster his address. Begin with the street.

You ask: "Where do you live?"
Child responds: "On Vine Street."

Gradually add the house number, city, state and telephone number..

By age <u>four</u> a child should be able to recite his address and telephone number.

This is very important for safety reasons. A lost little one who can give his name, address and telephone number will be more likely to get <u>home safely.</u>

At age <u>four</u> have your child draw a picture of his room or your home or apartment and then ask him to tell you a story about his picture. You write down the story he tells and read it back to him.

The parent can also do the same thing asking the youngster to draw a picture of himself and have him tell you a story about the picture. It can be fun to keep these pictures and stories and look back at them over the years.

Give your child praise and encouragement. Let your child know that he or she is respected as an individual.

Show by your interest that what your child does or says is valid and important.

A CHILD WHO IS RESPECTED WILL DEVELOP BETTER SELF AWARENESS AND SELF ESTEEM.

PASSAGE OF TIME

Teach your youngster about the passage of time. From <u>birth</u> talk about time, days of the week, holidays and dates.

At age <u>three</u>, make use of a calendar with your child. Pin one up and when holidays, birthdays or special events are forthcoming, show your boy or girl the current date and then show the date of the special event. Talk about how many days remain before the special event by counting the days on the calendar.

At the beginning of a new month, use cut-outs or stickers for special days.

Pin a picture of a birthday cake on the date of the child's birthday.

Do the same for the holidays.

Use the proper terms for the day of the week, the month, the year.

At <u>four</u> talk about each day of the week:

Today is Monday, the first day of the week. Discuss what usually happens in your family on Monday. What is the date? Today is Monday, September 1st, 1996. Talk about Saturday and Sunday being a weekend. It is a special time when some people do not have to work and children usually do not go to school.

You can start at an early age, <u>two or three</u> discussing hours. Tell your child that:

- Morning is when we get out of bed and have breakfast.
- Afternoon is when we take a nap.
- Night or evening is when we have dinner and then go to bed.

As the child gets older, <u>four or five</u>, you can discuss specific time. When it is

- 7:00 AM we get out of bed.
- 8:00 PM is when you go to bed.

When your son or daughter begins school, introduce the clock to show time. Your son or daughter will begin to understand the telling of time.

You can make some paper clocks which show get up time, lunch time, bed time and play time.

Part of understanding time is the passing of seasons. As you use the calendar with four and five year olds, talk about the four seasons of the year:

January through March is Winter

April through June is Spring

July through September is Summer

October through December is Fall

Discuss what happens in each season. If you live in an area where the seasons change, you will have natural weather experiences to discuss. If you live in a part of the country where the weather does not change much, you can use pictures, books and holidays to help your child understand the four seasons of the year.

Discussing the weather each day will not only help your child understand what is happening but may spark an interest in science. Remember to use the library. There are wonderful books about the weather and what makes it happen.

FAMILIARIZE YOUR CHILD WITH TIME, DAYS OF THE WEEK, MONTHS AND THE FOUR SEASONS.

Teach your child how to be a responsible and self-reliant person

STRUCTURE

Structure is very important to a child's well being, security, and readiness for school.

There should be routine in children's lives.

Try to have certain times for

- getting up
- going to bed
- playing
- eating
- homework
- television
- free time

Structure does not need to be, nor should it be, so rigid that there is no flexibility or creativity, but it is important. Youngsters who understand what is expected of them and when it is expected are much calmer and secure. They will be more open and ready to learn.

This became so clear during my teaching years. Each time our class was disrupted from its usual routine, the children became very restless, uncooperative, nervous, and even irritable.

They felt secure with routine and much more comfortable when they knew what we were going to do and when we were going to do it.

 **STRUCTURE AND ROUTINE WILL RESULT IN A MUCH CALMER CHILD.**

CHORES & RESPONSIBILITIES

A child who always has everything done for him and has no responsibilities grows up thinking the world and everyone owes him a living. Oftentimes, we feel we "do not want our children to suffer as we did" or "we want them to have more than we did." Modern society has proven this does not necessarily work. Give your child a head start in reality. You can start very early.

As soon as your child walks, have him pick up and put away toys. It is never too early for a youngster to learn about care and responsibility for belongings.

As your son or daughter grows, age two on, a chore suitable to the age will help the child begin to understand what it takes to be a member of a family, school classroom, and a member of society.

- A toddler can pick up toys and put them in a basket.

- A three year old can empty wastebaskets and help set the table.

- A four year old can help clear dishes.

- A five year old can make a bed.

By age <u>three</u> a child should have certain daily chores which teach responsibility and self-reliance.

Charts can be very helpful with routine and structure. For children <u>three and up</u>, you can use charts for chores, discipline and rules. Stars or stickers are terrific markers for a chore done, a behavior accomplished or a special rule followed. There can be rewards at the end of the day or week, depending on what you and your son or daughter decide upon when establishing the chart.

When structure, chores and discipline are used in the home, a child will find adjusting to school much easier. As classroom sizes grow, and even in smaller classes, there must be structure, discipline and even chores in order to have a good learning environment.

CHORES WILL HELP YOUR CHILD ADJUST TO THE RESPONSIBILITY OF BEING A STUDENT.

TV TIME

It is very, very important that you limit and monitor television time. Television is a passive activity. Children just sit and watch...probably watching material which is very inappropriate for their age.

There is very little imagination required and little conversation takes place when watching TV. Your child will be a better student if you regulate the amount of time spent in front of a television set.

If TV is a must, try to watch special programs together and talk about what was seen and what happened. There are some age appropriate and educational programs on television; however, they are few and far between.

Take the time to check out the programs and be aware of what your child is watching. There is no reason for a child to sit hour after hour in front of the television. Be aware of and control the time your child spends watching television.

Instead of watching television, help your children learn to be creative with their time. Suggest alternative activities. A few ideas are:

- Spend time with your child as he does homework; it might be a good time for you to read, pay bills, or write letters. Be a good model for your child.

- Cooking is a fun way to learn about measuring and fractions, planning menus, and learning about food groups.

- Play games which teach sharing and cooperation.

- Enjoy the great outdoors; nature is the world's largest playground.

- Learn to play a musical instrument; homemade instruments can be fun.

- Do arts and crafts; your child might have hidden talent.

- Reading is a good habit that can bring a lifetime of enjoyment.

- Gardening is delightful for children. Dirt in paper cups on a window sill can work for apartment dwellers.

- Watch birds build nests and then watch the eggs hatch. This can be a special way to introduce nature. Bird feeders on the deck or in the yard are fun.

- Use a tape recorder. Do you remember hearing your own voice for the first time?

Children are very impressionable and can be influenced in a negative way by television shows. They can be frightened by violence, they can be persuaded by commercials, and they will copy aggressive behavior. It can also affect their attention span. Children who sit hour after hour watching TV have a hard time when they must entertain themselves. A child, who has spent the first five years of life in front of a television, may find classroom life difficult.

If your children are addicted to television, try turning off the TV for just one night. In its place do some of the activities mentioned above or create some of your own. Gradually increase it to other nights.

Please note: It will be much easier if you limit TV at birth to avoid having to take it away later on.

> TURN OFF THE TV. IT MAY LEAD TO A HEALTHIER, HAPPIER LIFE FOR BOTH CHILD AND PARENT.

Treat your child as you would a best friend

SOCIALIZATION

Socialization is important to a youngster's development and readiness for school. Give your child ample opportunity to be with and play with other children. Being with other children will help your boy or girl learn:

- how to solve problems with others
- how to share with others
- the need for compromise with others
- how to relate to others
- how to take turns
- how to follow rules

The best way to teach the techniques of sharing, compromise, problem solving and relating to others is through example.

Show your children that you can compromise when you have difficulty with another person. Try not to argue in front of or with your children. Children who see their parents argue are often more insecure.

If you do happen to argue with another adult, explain to your child what is happening. If you must argue, then also show that you can solve the problem and makeup with the other person.

Teach your youngster there are better ways to solve a problem with another person. Compromise is a necessity and relating to others is something all of us must do.

Children do not come into this world with a natural ability for sharing. Teach sharing by explanation and example such as when you:

- let someone borrow your car
- when you lend an item to a friend
- when you give food to the homeless

Explain to your children how this is sharing.

Each of us must relate to other people every day. Make your children aware of the times you relate to others such as when you

- let someone go before you
- stand in line and wait your turn
- offer to help a friend

All of these concepts are important and critical to a child's well being when placed in a classroom of 25 to 30 other children.

Children must also learn that hitting, fighting and yelling never solves anything.

Sometimes adults think it is funny or cute when a small child uses a swear word. This will not be amusing or acceptable in school. Be a good example for your child and avoid the use of inappropriate language.

IF CHILDREN SEE VIOLENCE, THEY WILL LEARN TO BE VIOLENT

IF CHILDREN SEE KINDNESS, THEY WILL LEARN TO BE KIND

Learning to be a kind, respectful and caring person begins at <u>birth</u>. The social graces are important for your child's readiness, not only for school, but for his or her ability to get along in society.

This aspect of socialization can be an entire book in itself so some ideas are listed for your thought and consideration.

- Say please and thank you
- Be kind
- Do things for the less fortunate
- Wait your turn
- Respect others
- Have good table manners
- Write thank you notes
- Be polite
- Be a good listener
- Do not argue
- Share
- Resolve conflicts
- Do not interrupt
- Show appreciation
- Be responsible

YOUR CHILD WILL BE A MUCH BETTER STUDENT IF YOU TEACH SHARING, COMPROMISE, PROBLEM SOLVING AND RESPECT FOR OTHERS.

NUTRITION

Three well-balanced, nutritional meals are a must for all children. It is especially crucial when a child goes to school. A child who has had a good breakfast before leaving for school will be more alert and ready to learn. Youngsters who are hungry cannot concentrate and often are very restless. Students who have not eaten properly can be hyperactive for awhile and then get very listless.

Good nutrition is imperative in order for your child to do the activities discussed and, eventually, be a good student. Because young children are very active, they will probably want and need snacks between meals. Start your child on the road to good eating habits by providing fruits and vegetables as excellent snacks. Avoid "junk food."

Regarding healthy snacks, I would like to share an experience I had while teaching kindergarten. Many parents wanted to celebrate their child's birthday with a party at school. I allowed this just prior to dismissal.

The parent normally would bring cupcakes or a cake, candies, ice cream and other sweets. Much of this was left partially eaten on the children's plates.

One mother, who gave her daughter a party, brought wonderful fresh fruit which included pineapple, papaya and other exotic fruits. She also provided cut up fresh vegetables, nuts and cheese. I was shocked at the quantities she provided and was afraid the children would refuse to eat it. I was amazed at the results.

The kindergartners ate everything and very little was left over. Many of the children acted as though they could not get enough. They asked for seconds and thirds. It was a valuable learning experience for me.

We all like wonderful sweet treats; however, try to keep them at a minimum. You'll have a much healthier, happier, calmer child.

SLEEP

Keep an early bedtime for your child. A sleepy youngster will be restless, irritable and find paying attention very difficult.

A REGULAR BEDTIME SHOULD BE THE RULE.

Sometimes it can be trying and hard to get your child to agree. If you set up a bedtime routine and your child knows what is expected, you will have less hassle in the long run. After your child is in bed, as part of the bedtime routine, take a few minutes to talk about your child's day and read a short story. If your child knows you will spend a few moments together, he might be more willing to get into bed.

It will be much easier to awaken your child if he has had sufficient rest. This will be less trying on you especially if you are working. A child who is properly rested will be much more cooperative.

In the classroom, it was very obvious to me when a child came to school with just a few hours sleep. The child was listless, then restless, unresponsive and, sometimes, uncooperative. Very little learning could be expected.

After a good night's sleep and a healthy breakfast, your son or daughter will be much more ready to face the day, be happy and open to learning.

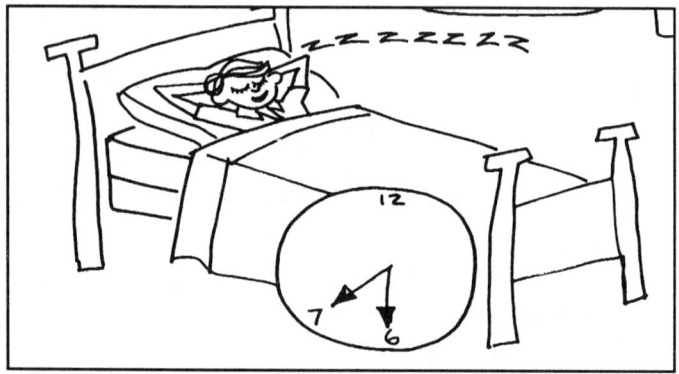

 PREPARING YOUR CHILD FOR SCHOOL WILL BE OF LITTLE VALUE IF YOUR CHILD DOES NOT GET ENOUGH SLEEP AND PROPER NUTRITION.

SCHOOL ATTENDANCE

When your child begins school, regular attendance is very important. The continuity of daily lessons, and a good daily routine will increase your child's chances for success.

If your youngster suddenly resists going to school, try to determine the cause. Possibly there has been a problem with another child or your boy or girl may have been scolded for something. Your student may have developed a learning problem in a particular area. There are many reasons why a child may suddenly decide not to go to school.

Do not give in just because he says he wants to stay home. Unless the student is ill, do not allow him to stay at home. Discuss the matter with your child and then privately with the teacher (not in front of the student). Once you have found the reason, take the appropriate action. If it turns out that there is a problem with the teacher or school rules; even if you disagree, do not let your child know. Work it out.

<u>Teachers and parents must be a team working together.</u>

If your child sees that you are concerned and will work with the teacher, he will be less inclined to take school lightly.

SHOW YOUR CHILD BY YOUR ACTIONS THAT YOU FEEL SCHOOL IS IMPORTANT.

Children should be eager to go to school

A READINESS SURVEY

The following questions will help you determine if your child is ready for school. Just because a child turns <u>five</u>, does not necessarily mean he or she is ready for school. Children develop and grow at different rates. You can use this check list to determine where your child is in his or her development. It will also give you more ideas for activities you can do to help your child be prepared for school.

PHYSICAL FACTORS:

* Will your child be 5 years or older before he/she begins kindergarten?
* Is your child's speech easily understood?

CAN YOUR CHILD....

* Pay attention to a short story when it is read and answer simple questions?
* Draw and color beyond a simple scribble?
* Tie a knot?
* Zip or button a coat?
* Fasten buttons he/she can see?
* Tell left hand from right hand?
* Be away from you for two to three hours without being upset?

CAN YOUR CHILD REMEMBER....

* Instructions and carry out 2 or 3 simple tasks after being told?
* His/her full name, address and telephone number?

CAN YOUR CHILD....

* Tell you the meaning of simple words like bicycle, apple, shoe, hammer?
* Count five objects?
* Put together a simple puzzle of five to ten pieces?
* Skip, hop, jump, gallop, run?
* Name and point to the parts of the body?
* Tell you why eyes and ears are needed?
* Name and point to the basic colors?
* Name and recognize any letters of the alphabet?
* Name and recognize any numbers from one to ten?

DOES YOUR CHILD....

* Like to look at books, magazines and newspapers?
* Pretend to read?
* Like to draw and write?
* Recognize a circle, square, triangle?
* Know concepts such as smallest, tallest, same & different?

HEALTH & SAFETY....

* Does your child normally sleep enough (anywhere from 8-10 hours)?
* Does your child eat well balanced meals?
* Does your child know how to use toilet facilities, Kleenex, drinking fountain?
* Does your child know how to cross a street safely?
* Does your child know rules about contact with strangers?
* Does your child recognize the dangers of broken glass, electric wires, throwing things?

SOCIAL COOPERATION....

* Does your child help with household tasks such as setting tables, feeding pets, putting away toys, maintaining his/her room?
* Does your child join cooperatively in play with other children?
* Does your child play games requiring taking turns and keeping rules?

DO YOU AS A PARENT....

* Watch TV with your child and ask questions about what you saw?
* Take your child to the zoo, on a train, to the movies (suitable for children), to the park, for a walk.
* Encourage your child to listen to and enjoy music, nature, art & science?
* Encourage your child to respect the environment?
* Encourage your child to respect all people?

HOME SUPPLIES

Having the following materials available to your child, will help him/her be more ready for school:

<u>**CHILDREN'S SAFETY SCISSORS**</u>: Allow your child to cut pictures from old magazines.

<u>**GLUE AND PASTE:**</u> Allow your child to glue or paste pictures cut from old magazines.

<u>**COLORING BOOKS AND CRAYONS:**</u> Allow your child to color. Do not place any pressure on the child for staying in the lines or choosing particular colors. Let them do their thing.

<u>**PENCILS:**</u> Allow your child to use pencils. Encourage proper grip, but DO NOT try to change a left-handed child to right-handed.

<u>**BOOKS:**</u> Give your child opportunity to look at books, as well as enjoy being read to by family members. Take your child to the public library. Teach proper care of books.

<u>**MATERIALS FOR COUNTING:**</u> Anything in the house can be used for counting. Count with your child. Count the dishes on the table, members in the family, toys, cars, etc.

PUZZLES: Try to have puzzles available. They are wonderful for visual perception development and hand-eye coordination.

BALLS: Give your child the opportunity to catch, bounce and throw balls.

JUMP ROPES: Help your child develop this skill. It will be difficult for some children, but just having a rope available and jumping rope with your child will help him/her learn this skill.

OLD TIRES: Good for hopping in and out. Great for obstacle courses.

CARDBOARD BOXES: These also make wonderful obstacle courses. Refrigerator boxes make terrific playhouses and club houses.

> GIVE YOUR CHILD EVERY OPPORTUNITY TO DEVELOP MIND AND BODY.

MORE WAYS TO HELP

Take a sincere interest and desire to aid in the progress of your child. Here are just a few suggestions for the many ways a parent can help a child. Be creative..you'll be surprised at what you can do.

MATH:

* Give your child games and playthings involving numbers and counting.
* Help your child understand numbers and their values...
    how much is ten?
    show me five?
    count the pennies?
* Let your child help you set the table, count the plates, silverware.
* Let your child help with cooking and simple measurements.
* Don't pass a dislike of math on to your child.

BOOKS:

* Make your house a house of books. Television <u>does not always</u> stimulate the mind in a positive way.
* Begin with books that will interest your child and are appropriate to the age.
* Take your child to the public library.
* Books make great presents.
* Have a special place for your child to keep books.
* If your child is looking at a book, try not to disturb.
* If you like books and if you read books, your child will probably like books.
* Show an interest in your child's reading. Encourage discussion.
* Subscribe to one of many wonderful children's magazines.
* Read and talk to (not at) your child.

HANDWRITING:

* Do not concern yourself if your child is left-handed. Do not try to change.
* Do not concern yourself with teaching your child to write, just avail him or her with the items listed earlier.
* Praise and encourage.

LIFE, COMMUNITY, WORLD:

* Familiarize your child with the neighborhood and community.
* Provide a map and globe of the world.
* Encourage hobbies.
* Help your child judge people individually and understand that differences are OK. Try to control your own prejudices in front of your child.

SCIENCE:

* Let your child be a collector; a little dirt is well worth encouraging curiosity.
* Talk about the weather and what makes it happen.
* Talk about nature, encourage bird feeding. Teach respect of the environment.
* Encourage your child to ask how and why.

HEALTH & SAFETY:

* Set a good example. Children love to be "copy-cats." If a parent observes good nutrition, safety, exercise...a child will copy.
* Send your child to school with a good breakfast. Provide a good lunch.
* Keep your child home when he/she is really ill.
* Provide a balanced diet. Food choices should not be left to the child. Discourage junk food.
* Establish an early and regular bedtime and stick to it.
* Have your child checked regularly by the doctor and dentist.
* Teach your child how to deal carefully and wisely with strangers, traffic, animals, unsafe areas.
* Help your child dress properly for school.

ORAL COMMUNICATION:

* Let your child talk; they have some very interesting things to say and should be heard.
* Children who hear proper language will use proper language.
* Explain and use the courtesies of speech. Discuss interrupting.
* Help your child learn how to give and take directions.

HOMEWORK:

* Provide a well-lighted, quiet place for homework.
* Set a regular homework time and stick to it.
* Show an interest and help but remember, homework is your child's responsibility.
* Let your child know you think school and homework is important.
* Check with the teacher if assignments are not clear.
* Encourage your child to do his/her very best. Neatness and care should always be encouraged.

Teach your child how to dial 911

GOOD LUCK!
YOU ARE YOUR CHILD'S BEST TEACHER

TEACH YOUR CHILD HOW TO BE SAFE

A MESSAGE FROM THE AUTHOR

Please don't be overwhelmed. Just keep in mind that it really is easy and uncomplicated to prepare your child for school.

It is my hope that this book will help you understand the importance of spending time with your child.

It is my hope that the examples given will inspire you to create many more activities for and with your child.

It is my hope that your child will be ready and excited about starting school.

While our lives are busy and complicated, our children deserve to have the best education possible.

Education starts at birth and in the home.

YOU CAN DO IT!!!

I welcome your comments.

Let's Begin
P.O. Box 77768
San Francisco, Ca. 94107

Be there for your child

ABOUT THE AUTHOR

Rose Marie Sicoli-Ostler is a graduate of the San Francisco public schools. She received an Associate of Arts Degree from City College of San Francisco and then a Bachelor of Arts Degree and Teaching Credential from San Francisco State College.

She taught kindergarten for several years in the Jefferson Elementary School District.

In addition to her teaching career, she was an Executive Secretary in the banking industry. Her other work experience includes obtaining a license and selling Real Estate.

She has tutored many students privately as well as for the San Francisco Educational Service. Currently she works as a volunteer tutoring both adults and children.

Mrs. Sicoli-Ostler lives in San Francisco with her husband.

Have fun